BOOK ANALYSIS

Written by Dominique Coutant-Defer
Translated by Rebecca Neal

Bonjour Tristesse

BY FRANÇOISE SAGAN

FRANÇOISE SAGAN

FRENCH WRITER

- **Born in Lot (France) in 1935**
- **Died in Honfleur in 2004**
- **Notable works:**
  - *Bonjour Tristesse* (1954), novel
  - *Il fait beau nuit et jour* (1979), play
  - *La Maison de Raquel Vega* (1985), short stories

Françoise Sagan, real name Françoise Quoirez, was born in south-west France in 1935 to an upper middle class family. She shot to fame on the literary scene with her first novel, *Bonjour Tristesse* (1954), which she wrote at the age of 18. She then published *Aimez-vous Brahms* (1959), *Wonderful Clouds* (1961), *The Still Storm* (1983) and many other novels, as well as around 10 plays and a fictional correspondence with the actress Sarah Bernhardt, which brought her continued success. With her passion for motorsport and her sometimes dissolute lifestyle, Sagan was widely talked about and came to symbolise an independent and carefree life. She died in Honfleur in 2004.

BONJOUR TRISTESSE

AN UNPREDICTABLE DRAMA

- **Genre:** novel
- **Reference edition:** Sagan, F. (2013) *Bonjour Tristesse*. Trans. Lloyd, H. London: Penguin.
- **First edition:** 1954
- **Themes:** sexuality, Oedipus complex, love, jealousy, suicide, manipulation

Bonjour Tristesse, which was published in 1954, takes its title from a line from a poem by Paul Éluard. It is a retrospective account by Cécile, the young narrator, of the summer that she spent on the Côte d'Azur the previous year. Her holiday begins pleasantly with her widowed father and his young mistress. They are living the joyful and carefree life they are used to when Anne, a poised and intelligent woman, shows up. A drama, stemming from the tensions between the characters, slowly develops, leaving Cécile facing a cruel dilemma.

SUMMARY

Cécile is a seventeen-year-old girl who left boarding school three years ago and lives with her father, Raymond. They lead a fairly superficial and lavish life, filled with flings and excursions. Raymond often brings his numerous lovers home for brief stays.

During the summer holidays, Cécile goes to a villa on the Mediterranean coast with her father and his current mistress, the young Elsa Mackenbourg. Anne Larsen, an old friend of her late mother, joins them later on. The young girl, who initially admires her, explains: "she spent her time with people who were sharp, intelligent and discreet, whereas the people we spent time with were noisy and insatiable". Anne quickly falls in love with Raymond and tries to win his affections and oust Elsa by any means possible. She also decides to teach Cécile and make her work, because the young girl failed her exams in June. This is not at all to Cécile's liking.

On the beach, Cécile compares Anne's perfect figure with that of Elsa, who is younger and who, moreover, cannot get a tan. She gradually thinks she notices that her father is trying to get closer to Anne by criticising, for example, Elsa's stupidity.

For her part, Cécile meets their young neighbour Cyril, a law student, whom she finds attractive, although she has always preferred older men. She very soon shares her first kiss with Cyril, which she regrets because she would rather have remained friends. She nonetheless thinks that he is well brought up and protective, and that she "would love to love him".

One evening, when they all decide to go to the casino in Cannes together, Anne is the most beautiful and elegant woman there, and Raymond compliments her. He shuts himself away with her. Cécile thinks that this behaviour is disrespectful towards Elsa, and is rude about it. Anne slaps her. Elsa, who has figured everything out, tells the young girl that she is leaving the villa and that she will miss the happy time she spent with them.

The next day, Raymond and Anne tell Cécile that they are getting married soon, which she is delighted about: she finally foresees a balanced life for her and her father. When the three of them make plans for a well-ordered life together, Cécile asks herself "did we ever believe in them?" She is, however, surprised that her father can leave his bohemian life behind so easily.

Unfortunately, the situation quickly changes. Anne catches Cécile and Cyril kissing and forbids the young couple from seeing each other again. Cécile is desperate and hopes that her father will help her, but he sides with Anne. Although the young girl is aware that Anne would be good for her and her father, she refuses to let them be at her mercy. She now sees Anne as cold and authoritarian. She then develops a strategy which aims to distance her from her father. She also decides to flout Anne's ban on seeing Cyril, and happily becomes his lover.

First of all, Cécile changes her way of life, going from exuberance to introspection. She becomes thinner and does not work. Anne thinks that she is turning herself into someone "sad and cerebral", which is not in her nature. She and Raymond pay extra attention to the young girl, aware that her despair is causing her to act like this. However, before long Anne is back to criticising how she is doing at school, which Cécile does not like at all.

Subsequently, Raymond tries to get closer to his daughter, who tells him that she will end up accepting Anne. He is thrown off balance and asks that, for all that, she does not renounce the previous life they shared, which he seems to miss a bit.

Some time later, Elsa, who is now tanned and in great shape, comes back for her suitcases. Although she feels ashamed of her Machiavellianism, Cécile decides to convince her to win back her father by persuading her to pretend to be in love with Cyril. When Raymond sees Cyril and Elsa together, he reacts quite violently. Cécile sees that her plan is working and decides to arrange for Elsa to meet her father by chance during a dinner. When he sees her, he is captivated by her beauty. Raymond's friends think that she is in love with Cyril, who is with her, which he is particularly angry about. However, once they have returned home he tells Anne that he loves her.

The narrator evokes her father, whom she judges to be materialistic and a dilettante, but also good and understanding. He is a wanderer, she says, and he would surely console himself if Anne left, although he does greatly admire her and no doubt sincerely loves her. But she wants her father back. She gradually lets the situation between them fester, when it would be enough to keep Anne away while her father shares a brief embrace with Elsa. If Anne found out about this fling, she would understand that she too had only been a passing affair for Raymond and would certainly break up with him.

This is exactly what happens: Raymond and Elsa finally meet in the village. Cécile feels overwhelmed by what she has set in motion. She is dismayed by the reaction of Anne, who has caught the couple and driven away from the house distraught. "Then all at once I saw that I had been attacking a living creature, a creature with feelings and not an abstraction", Cécile explains. Later, the father and daughter decide to persuade Anne to come back by offering her their apologies. However, they learn that she has just killed herself in the car. This suicide, made to look like an accident, appears to Cécile as the last gift that Anne has given them, sparing them from any guilt. Now Elsa and Cyril seem shallow to her.

After Anne's funeral in Paris, the father and daughter go back to their old life. Cécile embarks on a new relationship and Raymond has a new mistress. Nonetheless, the narrator, remembering the previous summer, experiences a new feeling: "with eyes closed, I greet it by its name, sadness: Bonjour tristesse". Thus ends the account of this decisive episode in her life.

CHARACTER STUDY

CÉCILE

Having left boarding school three years previously, Cécile is a wild-looking seventeen-year-old girl who cares little about her studies. She leads a relatively dissolute life in Paris with her father, which seems to suit her perfectly. However, Anne's arrival deeply shakes her beliefs and forces her to take a stand with regard to her father, who she adores, her young lover Cyril, who she does not know if she is in love with or not, and Anne, whose wisdom simultaneously attracts and repels her. As she leaves adolescence, she finds herself faced with a difficult choice between carrying on with her pleasant but somewhat shallow life, or embarking on a more constructive adult life. This dilemma drives her to develop a cruel game which she will not emerge from unscathed.

RAYMOND

Like his daughter, Raymond worships pleasure. Cécile says: "I have never loved anyone as much as him and, of all the feelings I experienced at that period, those I had for him were the most stable, the deepest and the ones I set most store by". An attractive man in his forties, he has made a series of conquests since he became a widower and, even though he is hopelessly frivolous, he is completely devoid of cynicism. He is also attracted by the stable life that Anne offers him and even goes so far as to ask her to marry him. However, he soon sinks back into his old ways, and ultimately his only emotional mooring point is his daughter.

ANNE

Anne is the same age as Raymond and works in fashion. She is an elegant woman, and the narrator highlights her "irony, effortlessness or authority", which do not stop her from being highly sensitive. Convinced that she could make Cécile and Raymond happy, she does everything she can to attach herself to them. However, she will ultimately be the victim of the Machiavellian plan thought up by the young girl, who she had tried to teach.

CYRIL

Cyril is a dark-haired young man who is "tall and could sometimes appear handsome, with a kind of handsomeness that inspired confidence". The narrator is immediately attracted to his balanced and protective character. He is a law student who lives in Paris and is spending his holidays with his mother in a villa close to that of Cécile. In some ways, he represents Anne's double in the narrative. Like her, he is sensible and is not afraid of long-term commitment, as he asks Cécile to marry him. However, she is just using him to carry out her plan.

ELSA MACKENBOURG

She is "a tall, redheaded girl, a mixture of playmate and sophisticate [...] very sweet, rather dim and quite unpretentious". She works as an extra for film studios, and Raymond points out her stupidity and superficiality in front of Anne. She is in love with Raymond, who only sees her as a temporary mistress, and prefers to leave him when she knows that he has been unfaithful. However, she enthusiastically takes part in Cécile's projects which allow her to win back her lover.

ANALYSIS

A PSYCHOLOGICAL NOVEL

The genre of the psychological novel first appeared in the 17th century with *The Princess of Cleves* (1678) by Madame de Lafayette (French author, 1634-1693), which takes as its subject the twists and turns of the heroine's passion for the Duke de Nemours, her doubts and her remorse. Based on psychological analysis, this kind of novel experienced a resurgence in the 19th century with novelists such as Henry James (English writer, 1843-1916), Virginia Woolf (British novelist, 1882-1941) and Colette (French writer, 1873-1954), who tried to get as close as possible to the inner lives of their characters, sometimes at the expense of the plot.

In particular, the psychological novel has the following characteristics:

- In most cases using an internal perspective, it intends to penetrate the secrets of individual behaviour by defining as closely as possible the actions, gestures, words, silences, feelings and emotions of the characters, taken individually or in their relationships with others;
- It describes in minute detail the psychological evolution of the characters over the course of the story: their states of mind undergo fluctuations and transformations, and it is this psychological movement that the novelist considers;
- Finally, the author's choice to prioritise the inner life of their characters necessarily affects the spatial and

temporal setting of the story which, in a way, reflects the state of mind of the characters.

Bonjour Tristesse (whose title also evokes a psychological state, namely sadness) resembles this category of novel in many aspects.

The psychological construction

The reader becomes aware of the action and the issues at stake through the "I" of the narrator and the precise observations she makes about herself and those around her. The network of characters is created starting at the focal point created by the "I": numerous internal monologues where the narrator dissects her state of mind, her hesitations and her remorse play a part in the construction of other characters who, refracted in her mind, gradually materialise before the reader's eyes and develop depending on Cécile's emotions. For example, the character of Elsa is initially presented by Cécile as a rather foolish and superficial woman, but as a result of the narrator's successive phases of reflection, she becomes a more sensitive person than she first seemed.

As such, self-analysis is mixed with the meticulous examination of others. Psychological stereotypes (the rebellious teenager, the middle-aged womaniser, the strong-minded woman, the disreputable woman) which are more nuanced than they first appear are put in place based on a plot that is on the whole quite trivial: a jealous daughter wants to keep for herself a father who is getting away from her. The character of Anne, whom it takes Cécile a while to grasp because of her complexity, illustrates particularly well the psychological work that the teenager has done to manage to get to the bottom of this woman's real feelings. Likewise, her own reactions often shock and unsettle her: does she want to continue with her old life or settle down? Does she hate Anne, or does she feel remorse at acting how she did towards her? What exactly does Cyril represent for her?

Psychology and action

The story takes on the appearance of a labyrinth in which the reader follows Cécile in the twists and turns of her confused and troubled thoughts. Moreover, the dynamic of the story comes more from these thoughts than from developments in the action, which only serves psychological ends. In Sagan's novel, it is not the action that causes psychological reactions, but the other way round: the psychology of the characters, and in particular of the narrator, sets the events in motion. Indeed, the novel opens with the reflections of the narrator, who claims that her temperament is prone to regret, boredom and frivolity. Her inner malaise, her Oedipal love for her father, her fundamental inability to make choices, and her sophisticated knowledge of her father's psyche guide the subsequent events.

A specific place and time

The action unfolds in July, close to a beach on the Mediterranean coast. Very early on in the story, the narrator highlights the importance of the elements: the constant rocking of the sea, as well as the blazing sun and its sweltering heat which sometimes numb her and stop her from thinking, but at other times stimulate her reflections. The narrator often links her psychological state to the environment: "We had sun and sea, laughter and love. Would we ever experience them again as we did that summer, with all the vividness and intensity lent to them by fear and remorse?"

The sun even becomes an essential participant in some scenes. In this way, when Cécile accepts Cyril's embraces, it is more because she is too lazy to fight against the heat and the blinding light than because she really desires him. In some respects, this behaviour brings to mind Meursault in *The Stranger* (1942) by Camus (French writer, 1913-1960), who commits a murder when he is blinded by the sun on a beach in Algeria. Furthermore, it is again the sun which cruelly marks the difference between Anne and Elsa at the start of the novel: Anne's skin effortlessly adapts to its burning rays, whereas Elsa's peels. Elsa only reappears once she has got used to the sun to become more beautiful in Raymond's eyes and seduce him again.

Likewise, the majority of the decisive exchanges between the three main characters take place outside, on the terrace of the villa, as if they were on stage at a theatre in ancient Greece. We can, then, make a comparison between the outcome of the novel and Greek tragedies, as both close with the death of a character. It is also worth noting that the only two social gatherings in the story (the night at the casino and the dinner at the restaurant) take place at night, as if only the main drama should unfold in the blinding light of the sun.

The comparison with the tragedies of Antiquity can also be

applied to the temporality of the story. Of course, the time of writing and reflection (indicated by the present tense) is spread over a relatively long time period of several months (since the narrator refers to "the summer in question" in the first chapter of the novel). Nonetheless, just as the setting of the events is circumscribed within a restricted area, the time that they cover is rather short: only a few weeks pass between the arrival of Cécile, Raymond and Elsa in the Midi region of France and their return to Paris. The pace seems to speed out of control in the last pages where Cécile, overtaken by the drama she has caused, abruptly loses her ability to reflect and manipulate and is unable to catch Anne, who suddenly dies in a car crash. This effect of sudden and unexpected acceleration of the action brings the novel even closer to the tragedies of Antiquity, which generally end abruptly.

A NOVEL TINGED WITH EXISTENTIALISM

If *Bonjour Tristesse* cannot be considered as a direct application of the theories of the existentialist movement, led by the philosopher Jean-Paul Sartre (French philosopher and writer, 1905-1980), Sagan, who was fascinated by Sartre's novel *Nausea* (1938) must necessarily have been familiar with the ideas of the philosopher, who was a major intellectual figure during the 1950s. Moreover, she met him on several occasions, and it must be noted that some aspects of her novels, and in particular *Bonjour Tristesse*, are connected to the major themes of existentialism:

- In 1943, Sartre published *Being and Nothingness*, in which he affirms man's existential solitude, left to his own devices without any external help (such as, for example, recourse to religion), whose life is marked by contingency and a lack of meaning. This solitude appears in *Bonjour Tristesse*. Cécile, left to her own devices, apathetic and idle, conceals the vacuity of her life by leading a frivolous and wild existence with her father or by sinking into a quasi-depressive state: "On the beach I did nothing but sleep and at mealtimes, in spite of myself, I maintained an uneasy silence". The only thing that anchors her is her body, celebrated and magnified in the novel, in which sexuality has an important place.

- According to Sartre, man is completely free to give whatever meaning he wants to his life – his destiny is in his own hands – and, consequently, he is responsible for his choices. The young narrator provides a good illustration of this complete freedom, which should be used wisely. In fact, Cécile tries to exercise this fundamental faculty, but her choices are often contradictory and changeable: she does not know if she wants to give in to Anne's vision of life or to continue her dissolute life with her father, or even to marry Cyril. Left entirely to her own devices, the teenager, facing the exhilarating and terrifying possibilities before her, is unable to manage her choices. She realises too late the tragic consequences that could result from them when, at the end of the novel, Anne dies suddenly, which brings her back to the emptiness of her own existence and the absurdity of her life.

THE RECEPTION OF THE WORK

From its publication, *Bonjour Tristesse* became a cult novel and the emblem of the entire post-war generation, although it also attracted criticism for certain aspects which were considered scandalous. Even today, the novel remains one of France's bestsellers and has brought its author wealth and fame. Shortly after this success, Sagan compared the fame this short novel had brought her at the age of 18 to an explosion.

The reason that *Bonjour Tristesse*, which was published in 1954, inspires such enthusiasm is because the work reflects certain aspects of the society of the time which had not until then been directly addresses in literature:

- Women's emancipation was starting to appear, but it was not necessarily viewed favourably. Sagan depicts an independent woman who is at ease with herself (Anne), and a disreputable young woman who has no qualms about jumping from one man to another (Elsa). The main character of Cécile is in a way the author's self-portrait, as a free young woman who has often been talked about because of her excesses of all kinds and who flaunts her taste for money and pleasure, which have earned her the nickname "charming little monster". In this way, in her first novel the 18-year-old author highlights the major change taking place in the 1950s in the middle-class environment she is from.
- The theme of sexuality (particularly female sexuality), which is central to the novel, contributes both to its

success and to the scandalous aspect for which some readers criticised the work. Indeed, the narrator refers without euphemism to the pleasure she experiences with Cyril, describes in detail Anne's expression when she gets out of Raymond's bed, and does not hesitate to call Cyril's mother, who has always lived off her husband's money, a "whore". Likewise, Cécile does not cast negative judgement on Raymond and Elsa's very free sex lives. Finally, not only does the author depict scenes which would be shocking to the right-thinking people of the time, but she also labels these situations using precise and sometimes crude terms.

Bonjour Tristesse therefore expresses the post-war generation's desire to live, thus helping this generation to identify with – and some critics to support – the heroes and situations of the novel.

Sagan has also been criticised for the narrator's clear-headedness regarding the situation with her father, who shows off his mistress and then takes in a friend of his dead wife, and for her choice to keep the tragic outcomes of this situation free of any pathos. In doing so she departs from traditional approaches to the novel, according to which events must be dramatised.

Her choice of psychological analysis, which in a way splits the character of Cécile in two, making her at once a participant in and judge of the situation, the Machiavellian plan that she sets into motion, and the right that the author gives to her character to hesitate and equivocate, all without demonstrating a clearly defined moral code, also contributed to the very varied reception of the novel.

FURTHER ANALYSIS

SOME QUESTIONS TO THINK ABOUT...

- Three women are at the centre of *Bonjour Tristesse*. Describe each of them and say in what ways they are similar or different.
- Explain what is specific about the spatiotemporal setting of the novel. What other genre can the story be linked to?
- In your opinion, why can Sagan's text be described as a psychological novel?
- What are the differences between the two male characters, Raymond and Cyril? What is the relationship between them, and how do they appear to the female characters?
- Can Cécile's attitude be described as Machiavellian? Justify your point of view.
- Why, in your opinion, could Sagan's novel have been considered immoral in the context of the 1950s?
- If this novel were published today, do you think it would be as shocking? Present your arguments.
- In what way does *Bonjour Tristesse* represent a break with the traditional novel genre (framework, action, characters, etc.)?

We want to hear from you!
Leave a comment on your online library
and share your favourite books on social media!

FURTHER READING

REFERENCE EDITION

- Sagan, F. (2013) *Bonjour Tristesse*. Trans. Lloyd, H. London: Penguin.